# Conjunctions

and

because

yet

but

although

unless

by Ann Heinrichs

Content Adviser: Kathy Rzany, M.A., Adjunct Professor,
School of Education, Dominican University, River Forest, Illinois

Published by The Child's World®
1980 Lookout Drive • Mankato, MN 56003-1705
800-599-READ • www.childsworld.com

Cover and page 1: Rawpixel.com/Shutterstock.com; 5: Eric Isselee/Shutterstock
.com; 7: istetiana/Shutterstock.com; 8: Vitalii Hulai/Shutterstock.com; 11: El
Nariz/Shutterstock.com; 13: apple2499/Shutterstock.com; 15: GGRIGOROV/
Shutterstock.com; 17: mTaira/Shutterstock.com; 19: MR. SUTTIPON YAKHAM/
Shutterstock.com; 22: Daleen Loest/Shutterstock.com; 24: George Rudy/
Shutterstock.com; 25: Pair Srinrat/Shutterstock.com; 29: Mariyana M/Shutterstock
.com

ISBN: 9781503832411
LCCN: 2018957532

Printed in the United States of America
PA02423

## ABOUT THE AUTHOR

Ann Heinrichs is the author of more than 200 books for children
and young adults. She has also enjoyed successful careers as a
children's book editor and an advertising copywriter. Ann grew
up in Fort Smith, Arkansas, and now lives in Chicago, Illinois.

# Contents

# CHAPTER ONE

# What Is a Conjunction?

[
**Definition: A conjunction is a word that connects two or more words or word groups.**
]

Conjunctions are like glue. They stick words together. We'd be lost without them! Just look at these examples. The orange words are conjunctions. Imagine each sentence without its conjunction.

**EXAMPLES**

Gorillas are huge **but** friendly.

We won the game **and** walked away with the trophy.

Pass the potatoes **unless** they're too hot.

Is Sparky in his doghouse **or** on my bed?

Until this young gorilla decides what to have for lunch, he will be hungry and his stomach will growl. How many conjunctions are in the previous sentence? If you found two, then you are right!

The conjunctions you know best are **and, or,** and **but.** But you'll soon see that there are plenty of others. **Although, because, until, besides, meanwhile,** and **otherwise** are all conjunctions.

Most conjunctions are just one word. However, two or more words can act together as a conjunction. **Even though, in fact, for example,** and **on the other hand** all act as conjunctions. Now let's have some fun with these useful words!

**DID YOU KNOW?**
The word *conjunction* comes from the Latin words meaning "to join together."

# CHAPTER TWO

# A Sandwich and a House? No Way!

[
**Definition: A coordinating conjunction connects words or word groups of the same type.**
]

Would you wear one shoe and an airplane to school? Would you carry a sandwich and a house in your lunch box? Of course not! You'd wear two shoes or two boots. Your lunch box might have a sandwich and an apple in it. You'd keep the same kinds of things together.

Coordinating conjunctions work the same way. They join words or word groups of the same kind. For example, they can join words, such as two nouns or two verbs.

Nothing goes together quite as well as peanut butter and jelly. The coordinating conjunction **and** helps bring them together!

## EXAMPLES

NOUNS **Can Sarah or Ryan come over today?**

VERBS **Nathaniel tossed and turned all night long.**

ADJECTIVES **Lizards can be green or brown.**

ADVERBS **Snoopy snored peacefully yet loudly.**

Coordinating conjunctions can join phrases too.

## EXAMPLES

**My goldfish jumped out of its tank and into my shoe.**
**Then it sprang out of my shoe and through the window!**

When joining words or phrases, coordinating conjunctions give us a shorter, easier way to say things. We don't have to repeat extra words. Just look at all the extra words in these examples:

---

**EXAMPLES**

**Lizards can be green, or lizards can be brown.**

**Snoopy snored peacefully, yet Snoopy snored loudly.**

**It sprang out of my shoe, and it sprang through the window!**

---

This lizard has green and black skin. The coordinating conjunction **and** helps us describe this reptile.

> **Definition: An independent clause is a complete thought. It has a subject and a verb, and it can stand alone.**

Coordinating conjunctions can also join independent clauses. Independent clauses are complete thoughts. They are equally important, and they can stand alone. Remove the conjunction, and both clauses still make sense.

---

**EXAMPLE**

**Brian has 40 baseball cards, but Eric has 50.**

**Brian has 40 baseball cards. Eric has 50.**

---

Usually you separate the clauses with a comma. However, if the clauses are very short, you don't need a comma.

---

**EXAMPLES**

**Roses are red and violets are blue.**

**Shape up or ship out!**

**Close the door but don't slam it.**

---

# CHAPTER THREE

# And . . . And . . . And . . .

> **EXAMPLE**
>
> **I'll have mustard and ketchup and pickles and relish and peppers and onions, please!**

Did you ever order a hot dog or hamburger this way? If you did, you must have run out of breath! You don't need to keep repeating the conjunction. Instead, separate the items with commas. Then put the conjunction before the last item.

> **EXAMPLE**
>
> **I'll have mustard, ketchup, pickles, relish, peppers, and onions, please!**

But wait! Sometimes you *want* to repeat the conjunction. You do this to make sure the listener gets your message!

> **EXAMPLE**
>
> **That terrier of yours just barks and barks and barks!**

Maybe you enjoy lots of different things on your burger, but you only need to use one conjunction when you order all of them.

# CHAPTER FOUR

# Laughing at Chimpanzees

[ Definition: A subordinating conjunction connects a main clause with a dependent clause. ]

**EXAMPLE**
I laugh **whenever** I see chimpanzees.

In the sentence above, **whenever** is a subordinating conjunction. We simply cannot do without this word! Remove the conjunction, and here's what you have:

**EXAMPLE**
I laugh. I see chimpanzees.

Fine. You're laughing. You see chimpanzees. But what's the connection? The missing link is **whenever!**

A subordinating conjunction connects two clauses. These two clauses are not the same kind of clause. One is the main clause. It's an independent clause that can stand alone. In the example on the previous page, **I laugh** is the main clause.

[

**Definition: A dependent clause has a subject and a verb. However, it's not a complete thought, and it can't stand alone.**

]

The subordinating conjunction introduces the other clause—the dependent clause. The dependent clause hangs on to, or depends on, the main clause. **Whenever I see chimpanzees** is the dependent clause.

Do you crack up whenever you see chimpanzees acting silly? The subordinating conjunction **whenever** links the reason you're laughing with the goofy chimps.

The dependent clause can come before or after the main clause. Either way, the conjunction must be *at the beginning* of the dependent clause. In the example below, the main clause is still **I laugh,** but there are two dependent clauses. One is before the main clause, and one is after it.

---

**EXAMPLE**

**Whenever I see chimpanzees,
I laugh until my sides ache.**

---

**WANT MORE?**

**Here are some common subordinating conjunctions: after, although, because, before, if, so, unless, until, when, whenever, while.**

---

**NOW TRY THESE!**

**Use subordinating conjunctions to connect these clauses. Point out which is the main clause and which is the dependent clause.**

1. The rooster always crows. The sun rises.
2. I'll be home at eight. I can get a ride.
3. I read comics. I howl. My friends cover their ears.

See page 32 for the answers. Don't peek!

We all know that roosters crow, and we also know that the sun rises. What's the connection? Roosters crow when the sun rises. The word when is the subordinating conjunction that helps us link the two thoughts in a single sentence!

# CHAPTER FIVE

# Conjunction Twins

[
**Definition: Correlative conjunctions are conjunctions that work together in pairs.**
]

Do you know any twins? If you do, you know they may not be exactly alike. But they do come in pairs. Correlative conjunctions are like word twins. They come in pairs too. Correlative conjunctions include **both/and, either/or, neither/nor, not/but, not only/but also,** and **whether/or.**

**HOT TIP**

Here's an easy way to remember that correlative conjunctions come in pairs. Part of the word *correlative* is *relative*. Just think of twins—they're relatives!

Like coordinating conjunctions, correlative conjunctions join things that are alike. They may join two words, two phrases, or two clauses.

**EXAMPLES**

**Both** parrots **and** sloths live in South America.

**Neither** zebras **nor** giraffes live in Asia.

**Father Goose is not a goose but a gander.**

I can't decide **whether** to do my homework **or** to go to bed.

James **either** makes a double play **or** hits a home run.

That ball landed **either** on the roof **or** in the pond.

Julie **not only** wrote the book **but also** directed the movie.

**Either** I get my pie, **or** I go home!

If we say that either Andy will get a home run or we will lose the game, we are using the either/or correlative conjunction.

# CHAPTER SIX

# Conjunctive Adverbs

[
Definition: A conjunctive adverb joins two independent clauses. It shows a relationship between the clauses and helps them flow smoothly.
]

Two independent clauses can stand alone, each as a complete thought. Then what does the conjunctive adverb do? For one thing, it helps you move smoothly from one idea to another. Things could sound pretty choppy without it!

**DID YOU KNOW?**

A conjunctive adverb is sometimes called an adverbial conjunction.

Conjunctive adverbs also show some special relationship between the two clauses. They might compare, sum up, or help make a point.

## EXAMPLES

I love cherries; in fact, I ate a whole bucketful.

Bozo had everyone in stitches. In short, he was a big success.

Our turtle started last; so far, he's still behind.

José is very athletic; his sister also loves sports.

Horses are fun to ride. I prefer camels, however.

As you see, there are two ways to separate the clauses. One way is with a semicolon (;). A semicolon works well when the clauses are short. You can also make the clauses into two separate sentences, with a conjunctive adverb in the second one.

This tortoise and rabbit are having a race; so far, it looks like they are tied! In this sentence, so far is the conjunctive adverb.

Where does the conjunctive adverb go? It can appear in many places. Often it's at the beginning of the clause it introduces. However, it can sometimes occur at the end of the clause—or even in the middle.

**WANT MORE?**

**Here are some common conjunctive adverbs:**
after all, again, also, anyway, besides, certainly, even though, eventually, finally, for example, furthermore, however, in fact, likewise, meanwhile, nevertheless, of course, otherwise, so far, therefore, though, thus.

**NOW TRY THESE!**

Here are four pairs of clauses. See how choppy they sound? Fix them by using a conjunctive adverb to connect each pair.

1. Sparky never bites. He growls a lot.
2. My feet aren't cold. It's still summer.
3. You have all the cards. You win.
4. Shut the door. Bugs will get in.

See page 32 for the answers. Don't peek!

# CHAPTER SEVEN

# Acting Like a Conjunction

Some words can be either prepositions or subordinating conjunctions. They are **before, after,** and **until.** How can you tell which is which? Just remember two simple rules:

1. Every preposition has an object.
2. A subordinating conjunction introduces a dependent clause.

---

**EXAMPLES**

| | |
|---|---|
| PREPOSITION | We're cranky **before** bedtime. |
| CONJUNCTION | We're cranky **before** we get our pizza. |
| | |
| PREPOSITION | Meet me **after** lunch. |
| CONJUNCTION | Meet me **after** I clean my desk. |
| | |
| PREPOSITION | I shall wait **until** noon. |
| CONJUNCTION | I shall wait **until** the cows come home. |

That is another word with many uses. It can be a pronoun, an adjective, or even an adverb. Just look:

**EXAMPLES**

| | |
|---|---|
| PRONOUN | That belongs to me. |
| ADJECTIVE | That dog belongs to me. |
| ADVERB | Its tail is not that long. |

We think that this dog looks sad. In this sentence, that is the subordinating conjunction because it introduces the dependent clause.

That can act as a subordinating conjunction too. It introduces a dependent clause.

**EXAMPLES**

Ms. Lopez announced that everyone could leave at noon.

Don't forget that we have rehearsal tonight.

Sometimes you can leave that out, and the sentence still makes sense.

**EXAMPLES**

Sophie knew (that) she'd written a good poem.

Be glad (that) you are here.

# CHAPTER EIGHT

# Because Why? Since When?

Some conjunctions can be tricky. They might trick you into using the wrong word. For example, you might use **since** when you really mean **because.** So let's be tricky too! Just follow some simple rules.

Use **because** to show a reason. **Because** answers the question "why?"

---

**EXAMPLES**

We haven't seen Grandpa **because** he's out of town.

Hannah has been wearing her new outfit **because** she loves it.

Skeeter doesn't bark **because** he's too tired.

---

Use **since** to show a certain point in time. **Since** answers the question "when?"

## EXAMPLES

We haven't seen Grandpa since he got home.

Hannah has been wearing her new outfit since she got it.

Skeeter doesn't bark since we changed his dog food.

## NOW TRY THESE!

Fill in the blanks with because or since.

1. We haven't eaten _____ the sun went down.

2. I couldn't sleep _____ the lights were too bright.

3. Poopsie keeps meowing _____ she sees a bird.

4. Elephants haven't come here _____ their water hole dried up.

See page 32 for the answers. Don't peek!

# CHAPTER NINE

# As If! Another Tricky Conjunction

Want another tricky conjunction? **As if!** Yes, it's true—**as if** is a subordinating conjunction. It introduces a dependent clause. **As if** answers the question "how?"

---

**EXAMPLES**

We screamed **as if** we'd seen a ghost.

It seemed **as if** class would never end.

It looks **as if** it's going to rain.

---

Have you ever felt as if your school day would never end? The subordinating conjunction as if introduces a dependent clause.

What's the tricky part? **As if** is often confused with **like.** However, **like** is a preposition. As with all prepositions, **like** only has an object. It doesn't introduce a clause.

## EXAMPLES

WRONG    It seemed **like** class would never end.

RIGHT    It seemed **like** a movie.

WRONG    It looks **like** it's going to rain.

RIGHT    It looks **like** a trick.

WRONG    We screamed **like** we'd seen a ghost.

RIGHT    We screamed **like** fire engines.

## NOW TRY THESE!

### Fill in the blanks with as if or like.

1. Act _____ a gorilla.

2. Act _____ you want to be chosen.

3. I ran _____ tigers were chasing me.

4. I ran _____ the wind.

See page 32 for the answers. Don't peek!

# CHAPTER TEN

# Just for Fun: Sloppy Conjunctions

**EXAMPLES**

Jennifer is friendly **and** Jennifer is polite.

Scooter is black **and** Scooter is gray.

That mouse grabbed the cheese **and** grabbed the nuts!

Whew! That's a lot of extra words! Remember the coordinating conjunctions? They can give us a shorter, easier way to say things. We don't have to repeat extra words. Get rid of the extra words, and the meaning stays the same.

**QUICK FACT**

And, but, **and** or are the most common coordinating conjunctions.

**EXAMPLES**

Jennifer is friendly **and** polite.

Scooter is black **and** gray.

That mouse grabbed the cheese **and** the nuts!

Now look at these examples:

> **EXAMPLES**
>
> Eat these brownies while they're nice and hot.
>
> I'll try and get a B on my math test.
>
> We'll stop reading when we're good and ready!

Are these shorter and easier ways to say something? Let's find out by adding in the extra words:

> **EXAMPLES**
>
> Eat these brownies while they're nice and while they're hot.
>
> I'll try and I'll get a B on my math test.
>
> We'll stop reading when we're good and when we're ready!

Oops! These sentences are not what we mean at all! What's the problem? We got a little sloppy with the coordinating conjunction **and.** It didn't pass the "extra words" test!

It's easy and fun to say **nice and hot, try and get,** and **good and ready.** But remember—these words don't say what you really mean. How can you fix them? Just remove the sloppy conjunction and use different words!

**EXAMPLES**
Eat these brownies while they're really hot.
I'll try to get a B on my math test.
We'll stop reading when we're absolutely ready!

# Fun with Conjunctions

Subordinating conjunctions can completely change the meaning of a sentence. Read each of these sentences twice, using a different conjunction each time. Tell how the meaning is different each time.

I want to swim **until/while** I eat lunch.

Emily will go **because/unless** I am going.

Brush your teeth **before/after** you go to bed.

**Although/Because** he is a clown, he is sad.

My hands get dirty **if/so** I wash them.

# How to Learn More

## IN THE LIBRARY

Atwood, Megan, and Estudio Haus (illustrator). *Cailyn and Chloe Learn about Conjunctions*. Chicago, IL: Norwood House Press, 2015.

Cleary, Brian P., and Brian Gable (illustrator). *But and For, Yet and Nor: What Is a Conjunction?* Minneapolis, MN: Millbrook Press, 2014.

Meister, Cari, and Holli Conger (illustrator). *Pepperoni or Sausage? A Book about Conjunctions*. Mankato, MN: Amicus, 2016.

Rajczak, Kristen. *Conjunctions with Your Friends*. New York, NY: Gareth Stevens, 2013.

## ON THE WEB

Visit our website for links about conjunctions:
**childsworld.com/links**

*Note to Parents, Teachers, and Librarians: We routinely verify our web links to make sure they are safe and active sites. So encourage your readers to check them out!*

# Index

# Answers

**page 14**

There are many possible answers.
Here are some suggestions.
*(The main clause is in italics.)*

1. *The rooster always crows*
   before the sun rises.
2. *I'll be home at eight* if I can get
   a ride.
3. When I read comics, *I howl*
   until my friends cover their ears.

**page 20**

There are many possible answers.
Here are some suggestions:

1. Sparky never bites;
   nevertheless, he growls a lot.
2. My feet aren't cold. After all,
   it's still summer.
3. You have all the cards;
   therefore, you win.
4. Shut the door; otherwise,
   bugs will get in.

**page 24**

1. since
2. because
3. because
4. since

**page 26**

1. like
2. as if
3. as if
4. like